NEXT STATION

STARTER S

STUDENT'S BOOK

Amanda Cant / Mary Charrington
Sarah Elizabeth Sprague

CONTENTS

| PAGES 4-5 | **Icons** | PAGES 6-7 | **World Map** |

PAGES 8-17

VOCABULARY
hello, goodbye, bye, yes, no

one, two, three, four, five, six, seven, eight, nine, ten

GRAMMAR
I'm (Roberto).

I'm (six).

FEATURES
The World
World Music Song: Welcome to Next Station

PAGES 18-27

VOCABULARY
pencil, eraser, pen, pencil case, ruler

backpack, chair, glue stick, crayon, book

GRAMMAR
It's a (pencil).
It's an (eraser).

one (book)
two (books)

FEATURES
Country: South Korea
World Music Song: Welcome to Korea

| PAGES 28-29 | **Progress Check Units 1 & 2** | PAGES 30-31 | **Steam Challenge 1** |

PAGES 32-41

VOCABULARY
red, blue, yellow, pink, green

gray, black, white, brown, orange

GRAMMAR
It's (red).
My (pencil) is (pink).

FEATURES
Country: Brazil
World Music Song: Welcome to Brazil

PAGES 42-51

VOCABULARY
ball, puppet, guitar, scooter, teddy bear

doll, yo-yo, bike, kite, video game

GRAMMAR
I have a (puppet).

I have a (red) (kite).

FEATURES
Country: Mexico
World Music Song: Welcome to Mexico

| PAGES 52-53 | **Progress Check Units 3 & 4** | PAGES 54-55 | **Steam Challenge 2** |

PAGES 56-65

VOCABULARY
head, arms, hands, legs, feet

eyes, ears, nose, mouth, hair

GRAMMAR
This is my (head).
These are my (arms).
I have (a nose).
I have (two eyes).

FEATURES
Country: Ireland
World Music Song: Welcome to Ireland

2

UNIT 6 — PAGES 66-75

VOCABULARY: mom, dad, grandma, grandpa, sister, brother; big, small, old, young

GRAMMAR: This is my (mom). My (grandma) is (old).

FEATURES: **Country:** Vietnam **World Music Song:** Welcome to Vietnam

PAGES 76-77 **Progress Check Units 5 & 6** PAGES 78-79 **Steam Challenge 3**

UNIT 7 — PAGES 80-89

VOCABULARY: lion, giraffe, elephant, monkey, zebra; goat, donkey, hen, cow, dog

GRAMMAR: It's (brown) and (yellow). They're (hens).

FEATURES: **Country:** Botswana **World Music Song:** Welcome to Botswana

UNIT 8 — PAGES 90-99

VOCABULARY: hat, shirt, skirt, sweater, pants; T-shirt, dress, socks, shoes, shorts

GRAMMAR: It's my (hat). They're my (pants). It's your (hat). They're your (shoes).

FEATURES: **Country:** Peru **World Music Song:** Welcome to Peru

PAGES 100-101 **Progress Check Units 7 & 8** PAGES 102-103 **Steam Challenge 4**

UNIT 9 — PAGES 104-113

VOCABULARY: rice, orange, banana, fish, salad; pizza, pasta, fries, juice, water

GRAMMAR: I like (salad). I don't like (fish). Do you like (pasta)? Yes, I do. No, I don't.

FEATURES: **Country:** Italy **World Music Song:** Welcome to Italy

UNIT 10 — PAGES 114-123

VOCABULARY: bedroom, living room, bathroom, kitchen, yard; table, TV, closet, bed, sofa

GRAMMAR: I'm in the (bedroom). There's a (bed) in the (bedroom).

FEATURES: **Country:** USA **World Music Song:** Welcome to USA

PAGES 124-125 **Progress Check Units 9 & 10** PAGES 126-127 **Steam Challenge 5**

PAGE 128 **MY PICTURE DICTIONARY**

· ICONS ·

 WRITE / NUMBER

 COLOR

 CIRCLE / DRAW

 MATCH / FOLLOW

 POINT

 SAY / TELL

 SING

 COUNT

 ACT

 PLAY

 MAKE

 LISTEN

 WORLD MUSIC

 BE sociable and creative. Know yourself!

 THINK critically when you use information!

 LEARN to do things by yourself. Learn how to learn!

 COLLABORATE / COMMUNICATE with others. Teamwork is cool!

 ACT respectfully, be tolerant, and friendly!

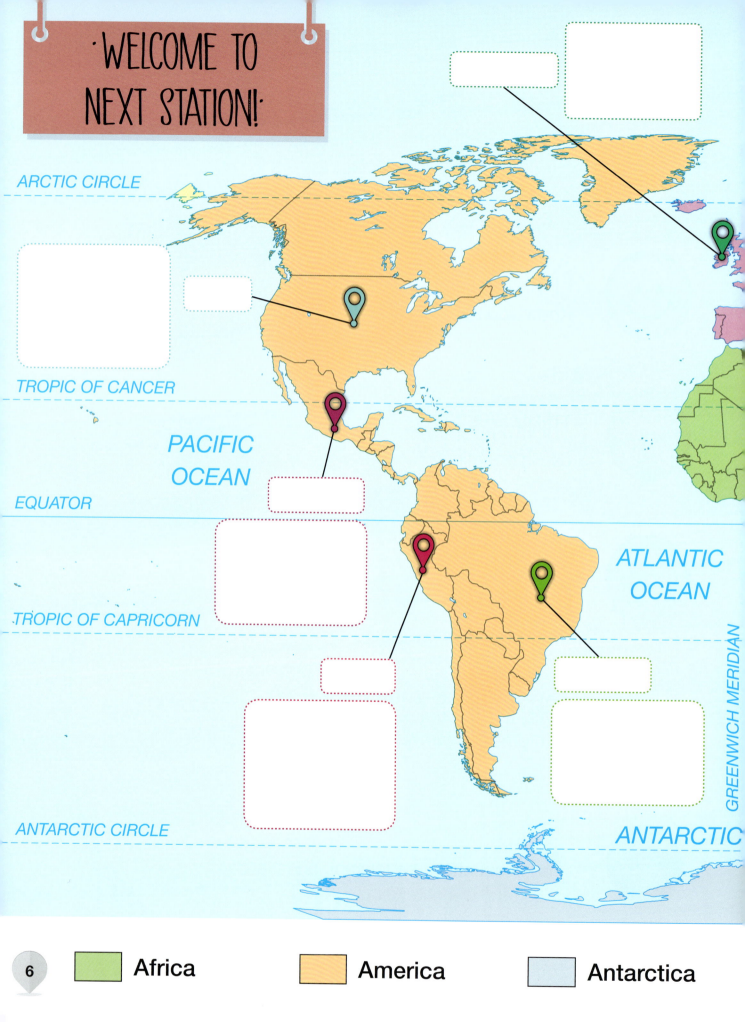

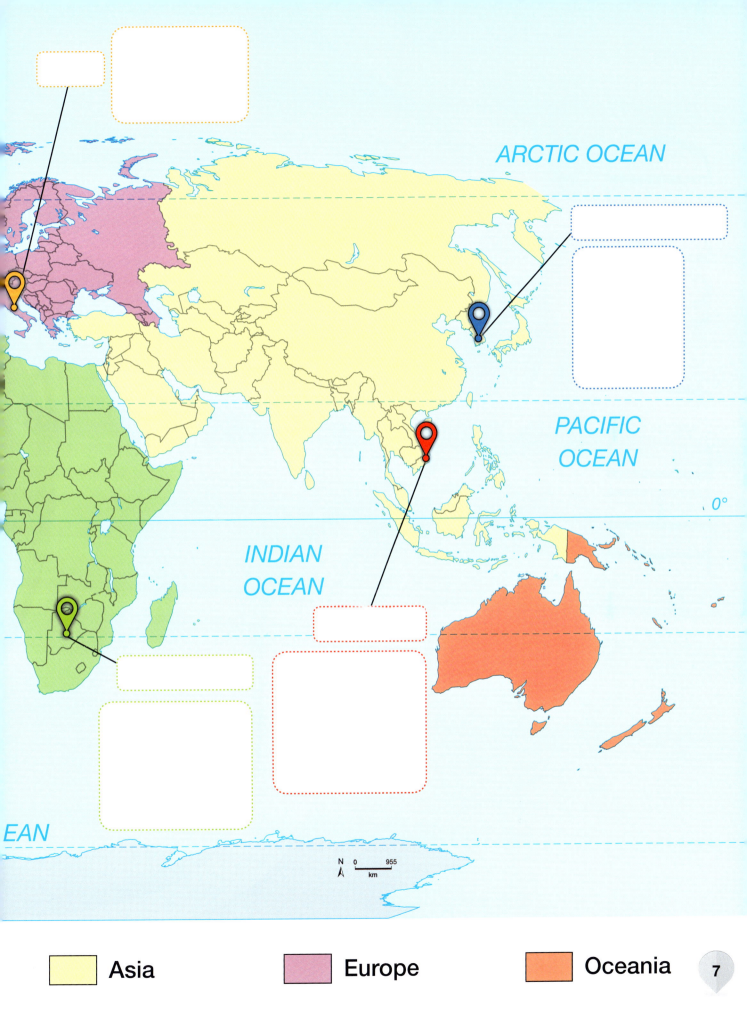

THE WORLD

UNIT 1

 TRACK 2

Sing the song.

WORKBOOK
page 3

Lesson 1

· VOCABULARY ·

TRACK 3

1 Listen and point.

TRACK 4

2 Listen and match.

10

WORKBOOK page 4

Lesson 2

GRAMMAR
I'm (Roberto).

TRACK 5
 1 Listen and point.

 2 Say *Hello* and *Goodbye*.

WORKBOOK page 5

11

Lesson 3

PRACTICE

 1 Listen and say.

 2 Listen and play.

WORKBOOK page 6

Lesson 4

· VOCABULARY ·

TRACK 8
 1 Listen and say.

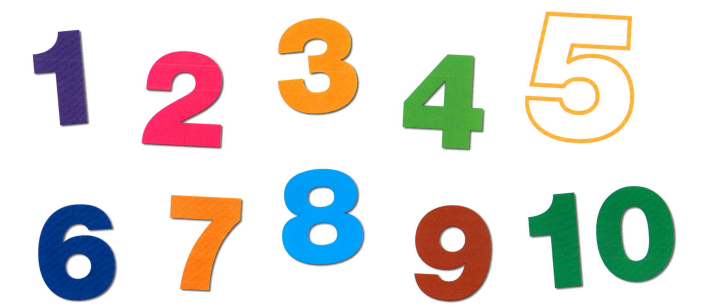

TRACK 9
 2 Sing and act out.

WORKBOOK page 7

MY PICTURE DICTIONARY page 129

13

Lesson 5

TRACK 10

1 Listen and point.

GRAMMAR

I'm (six).

 2 Follow and say.

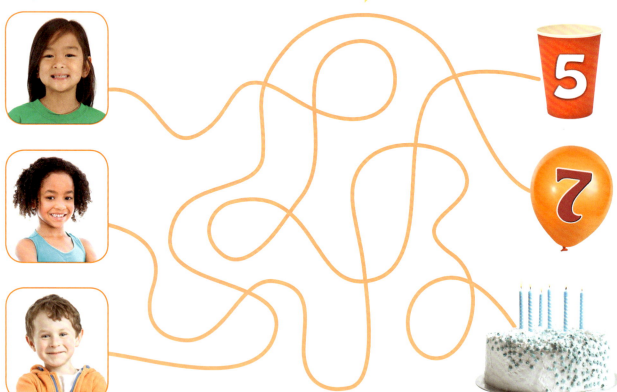

WORKBOOK page 8

Lesson 6

PRACTICE

 1 Match and color.

2 Write and say.

__ 2 3 4 __ 6 __ 8 __ 10

Lesson 7

STORY TIME

TRACK 11

 1 Listen and point.

 2 Act out.

 3 Circle the value.

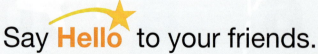 Say **Hello** to your friends.

16

WORKBOOK page 10

Lesson 8 · CRAFT TIME·

1 Make a people chain.

2 Show and say.

Hello

WORKBOOK page 83

UNIT 2 · SOUTH KOREA ·

WELCOME TO SOUTH KOREA

TRACK 12

Sing the song.

WORKBOOK page 11

Lesson 1

VOCABULARY

TRACK 13

1 Listen and point.

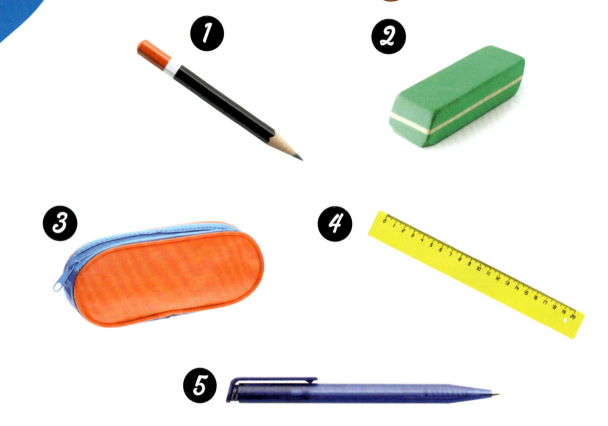

TRACK 14

2 Listen and number.

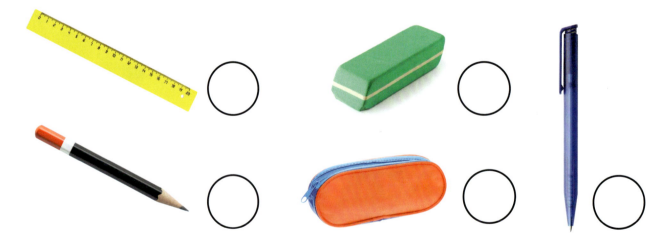

WORKBOOK
page 12

Lesson 2

 TRACK 15

1 Listen and point.

GRAMMAR
It's a (pencil).
It's an (eraser).

2 Draw and say.

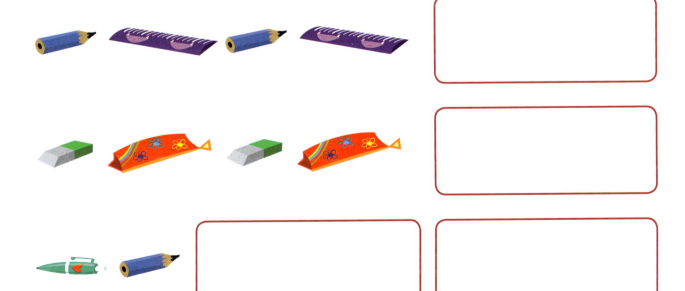

WORKBOOK page 13

21

Lesson 4 ·VOCABULARY·

 1 Listen and point.

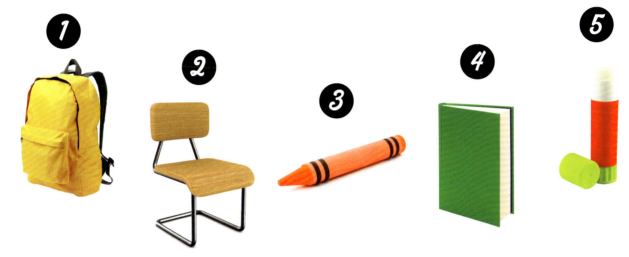

 2 Sing and act out.

Lesson 5

 1 Listen and point.

GRAMMAR
one (book)
two (books)

 2 Play and say.

WORKBOOK page 16

Lesson 6

 1 Count and write.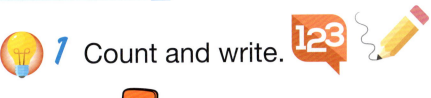

·PRACTICE·

 2 Say.

Lesson 7

TRACK 19

 1 Listen and point.

 2 Act out.

 3 Circle the value.

 of your school things.

26

WORKBOOK page 18

Lesson 8

· CRAFT TIME ·

1 Make pencil puppets.

2 Act out the story.

WORKBOOK page 85

UNIT 1

PROGRESS CHECK

1 Say and color.

TRACK 20

2 Listen and number.

 STICKERS   PASSPORT Page 2

PROGRESS CHECK

1 Say and color.

 2 Listen and number.

TEAM NAME

❶ Get materials.

❷ Cut the paper.

 **CHALLENGE 1**

· BUILD AN AIRPLANE ·

 SOUTH KOREA

3 Make circles and tape.

4 Tape straws to circles.

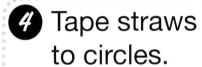

5 Fly!

6 Draw your airplane.

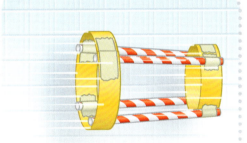

Super Star Challenge
Build an airplane with 1 straw.

 TEAMWORK ★★★★★

31

BRAZIL

UNIT 3

 Sing the song.

WORKBOOK
page 19

UNIT 3 Lesson 1

VOCABULARY

TRACK 23
 1 Listen and point.

TRACK 24
 2 Listen and color.

34

WORKBOOK page 20

Lesson 2

GRAMMAR

It's (red).

TRACK 25

1 Listen and point.

❶  ❷

2 Circle and say.

WORKBOOK page 21

35

Lesson 3

·PRACTICE·

1 Color.

1  2  3  4  5

TRACK 26

 2 Listen and point.

Lesson 4 VOCABULARY

 1 Listen and point.

 2 Listen and color.

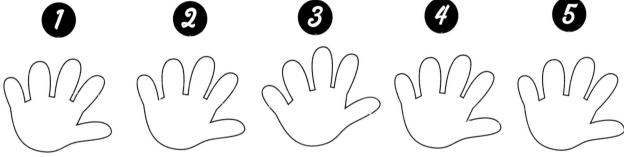

 3 Sing and act out.

37

Lesson 5

GRAMMAR
My (pencil) is (pink).

TRACK 30

1 Listen and point.

2 Play and say.

WORKBOOK page 24

38

Lesson 6

 1 Follow and color.

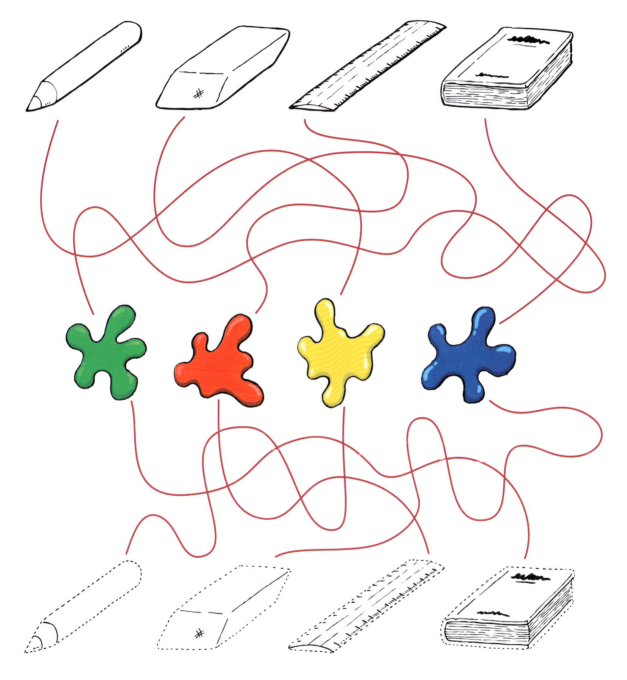

 2 Play a game.

UNIT 3

Lesson 7

STORY TIME

TRACK 31

1 Listen and point.

2 Act out.

3 Circle the value.

Express your opinions.

Lesson 8

CRAFT TIME

1 Make a heart.

2 Say.

· MEXICO ·

MEXICO

UNIT

4

TRACK 32

Sing the song.

WORKBOOK
page 27

Lesson 1

· VOCABULARY ·

TRACK 33

1 Listen and point.

2 Complete and say.

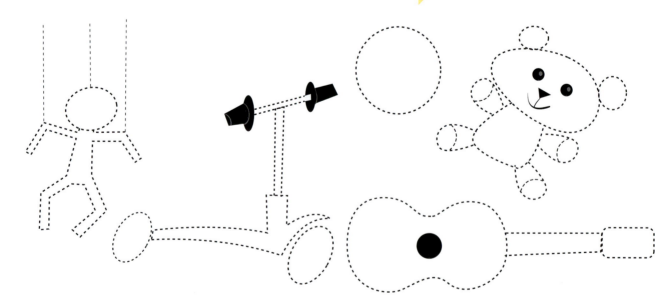

Lesson 2

GRAMMAR
I have a (puppet).

TRACK 34

1 Listen and point.

TRACK 35

2 Listen and match.

WORKBOOK page 29

45

UNIT 4 — Lesson 3

PRACTICE

TRACK 36

1 Listen and circle.

2 Draw and say.

WORKBOOK page 30

Lesson 4 ·VOCABULARY·

TRACK 37

1 Listen and point.

TRACK 38

2 Listen and number.

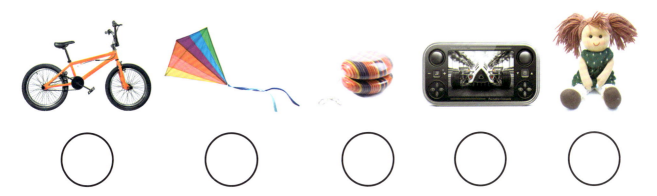

◯ ◯ ◯ ◯ ◯

TRACK 39

3 Sing and act out.

WORKBOOK page 31

MY PICTURE DICTIONARY page 130

47

Lesson 5

TRACK 40

1 Listen and point.

· GRAMMAR ·

I have a (red) (kite).

1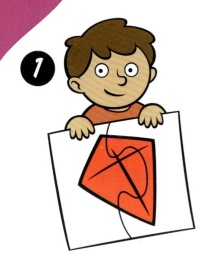
2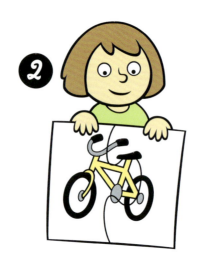
3

TRACK 41

2 Listen and match.

1
2
3
4

48

WORKBOOK
page 32

Lesson 6

·PRACTICE·

TRACK 42

1 Listen and color.

2 Say.

Lesson 7

STORY TIME

TRACK 43

 1 Listen and point.

 2 Act out.

 3 Circle the value.

 together.

50

WORKBOOK page 34

Lesson 8

·CRAFT TIME·

1 Make a toy.

2 Play and say.

51

PROGRESS CHECK

1 Say and color.

TRACK 44
 2 Listen and number.

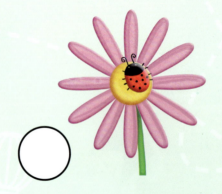

 STICKERS
 PASSPORT Page 6

52

UNIT 4

· PROGRESS CHECK ·

1 Say and color.

TRACK 45

2 Listen and number.

BRAZIL

TEAM NAME

① Get materials.

② Copy and color your bat. Then cut.

54

CHALLENGE 2

MAKE A FLYING FREE-TAILED BAT

MEXICO

3 Tape cap to bat.

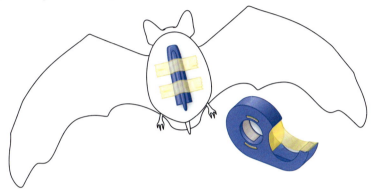

4 Insert straw.

5 Blow and fly!

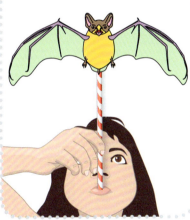

6 Draw your bat in action.

Super Star Challenge
Make a bat cave colony.

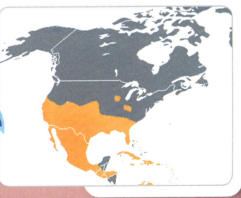

TEAMWORK ★★★★★

IRELAND

UNIT 5

TRACK 46 Sing the song.

WORKBOOK
page 35

Lesson 1

TRACK 47

1 Listen and point.

TRACK 48

2 Listen and draw. ✏️

Lesson 2

GRAMMAR
This is my (head).
These are my (arms).

TRACK 49

1 Listen and say.

TRACK 50

2 Listen and circle.

WORKBOOK
page 37

Lesson 3

PRACTICE

TRACK 51
 1 Listen and color.

 2 Act out and say.

WORKBOOK
page 38

Lesson 4

· VOCABULARY ·

TRACK 52

1 Listen and point.

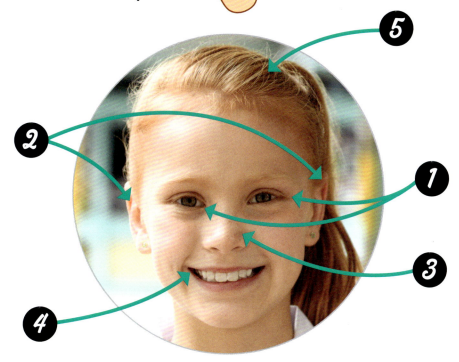

TRACK 53

2 Sing and act out.

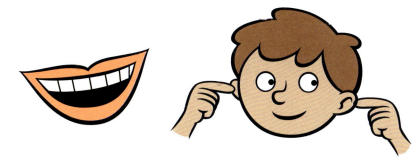

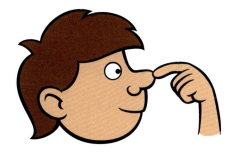

Lesson 5

TRACK 54

 1 Listen and draw.

GRAMMAR
I have (a nose).
I have (two eyes).

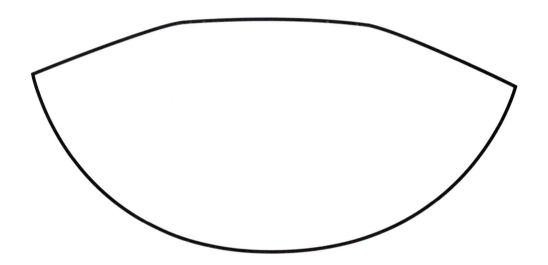

TRACK 55

 2 Listen and say *Yes* or *No*.

62

WORKBOOK
page 40

Lesson 6

  1 Listen and match.

 2 Act out and say.

Lesson 7

 STORY TIME

TRACK 57

 1 Listen and point.

 2 Act out.

 3 Circle the value.

 your friends.

64

WORKBOOK page 42

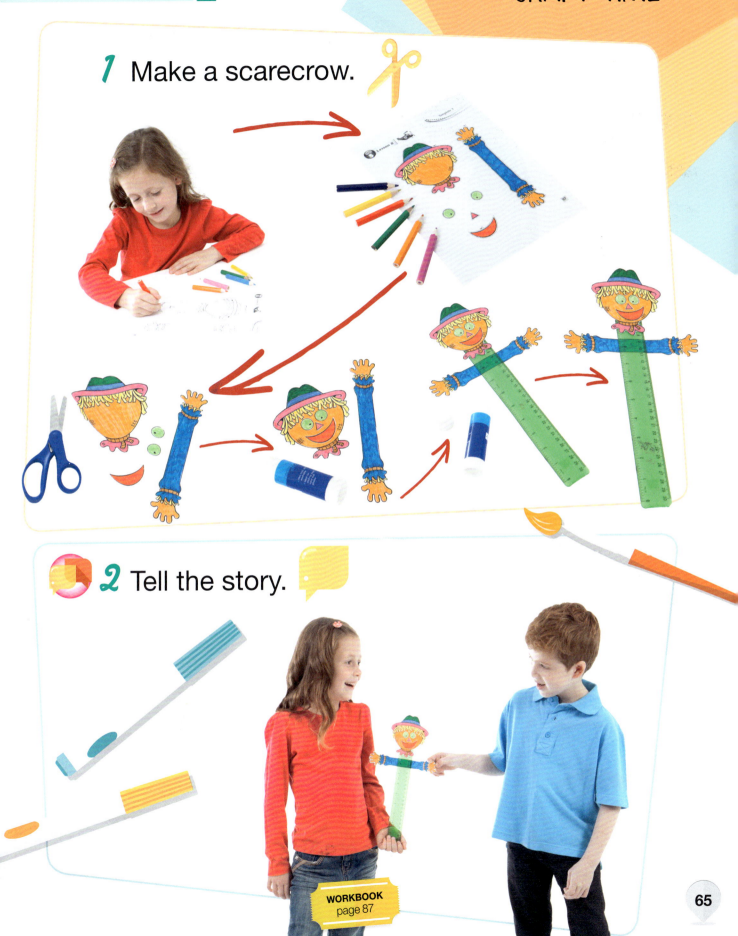

WORKBOOK
page 43

Lesson 1

· VOCABULARY ·

TRACK 59

1 Listen and point.

1 2 3 4 5 6

2 Match and say.

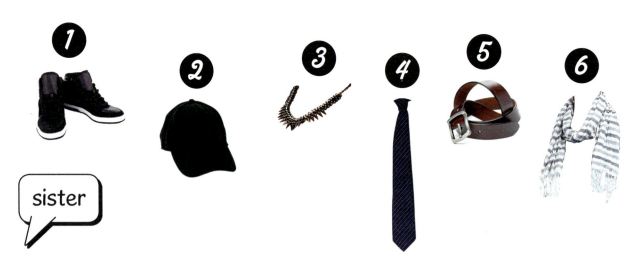

1 2 3 4 5 6

sister

WORKBOOK
page 44

68

Lesson 2

GRAMMAR

This is my (mom).

TRACK 60

1 Listen and point.

TRACK 61

2 Listen and match.

WORKBOOK
page 45

69

Lesson 3

PRACTICE

1 Draw your family.

 2 Show and say.

WORKBOOK page 46

Lesson 4 ·VOCABULARY·

TRACK 62

1 Listen and point.

TRACK 63

 2 Sing and act out.

Lesson 5

 1 Listen and point.

GRAMMAR
My (grandma) is (old).

 2 Listen and circle.

WORKBOOK page 48

Lesson 6 PRACTICE

 1 Listen and circle.

 2 Say and act out.

WORKBOOK page 49

 **Lesson 7**

·STORY TIME·

TRACK 67

 1 Listen and point.

 2 Act out.

 3 Circle the value.

 **Help** your family.

74

WORKBOOK page 50

Lesson 8

· CRAFT TIME ·

1 Make a family poster.

2 Show and say.

PROGRESS CHECK

1 Say and color.

TRACK 68

2 Listen and number.

PROGRESS CHECK

1 Say and color.

 TRACK 69

2 Listen and number.

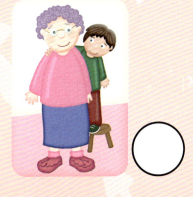  

STICKERS PASSPORT Page 12

77

IRELAND

STEAM

TEAM NAME

❶ Get materials.

❷ Mix sand and cornstarch.

CHALLENGE 3

BUILD A CASTLE

VIETNAM

3 Mix dish soap and water.

4 Mix all ingredients.

5 Wait 10 minutes then build.

6 Draw your castle.

Super Star Challenge — Design a door.

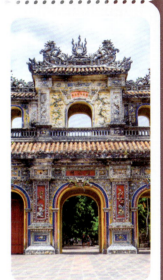
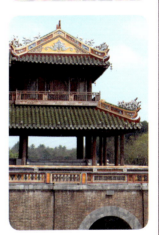

TEAMWORK ★★★★★

79

BOTSWANA

UNIT 7

TRACK 70
Sing the song.

WORKBOOK
page 51

Lesson 1

· VOCABULARY ·

TRACK 71

 1 Listen and point.

1   2   3   4   5

2 Match and say.

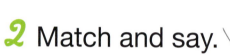

82

WORKBOOK page 52

Lesson 2

· GRAMMAR ·

It's (brown) and (yellow).

TRACK 72

1 Listen and point.

TRACK 73

2 Listen and color.

WORKBOOK
page 53

83

Lesson 3

·PRACTICE·

 1 Listen and number.

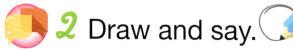 2 Draw and say.

WORKBOOK
page 54

Lesson 4 · VOCABULARY ·

TRACK 75

1 Listen and point.

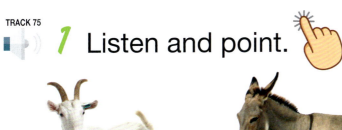

TRACK 76

2 Match and sing.

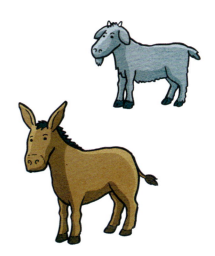

WORKBOOK page 55

MY PICTURE DICTIONARY page 132

85

Unit 7 · Lesson 5

GRAMMAR
They're (hens).

TRACK 77

1 Listen and match.

2 Match and say.

86

WORKBOOK page 56

Lesson 6

 1 Draw and say.

· PRACTICE ·

87

Lesson 7

STORY TIME

TRACK 78

 1 Listen and point.

 2 Act out.

 3 Circle the value.

 other people's things.

Lesson 8

· CRAFT TIME ·

1 Make a goat.

2 Act out the story.

WORKBOOK page 89

PERU

UNIT 8

 Sing the song.

WORKBOOK
page 59

Lesson 1

· VOCABULARY ·

 TRACK 80

1 Listen and point.

2 Complete and say.

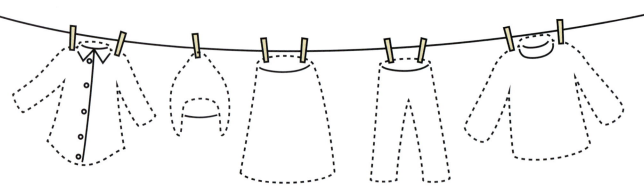

WORKBOOK page 60

Lesson 2

GRAMMAR
It's my (hat).
They're my (pants).

TRACK 81
 1 Listen and point.

TRACK 82
 2 Listen and match.

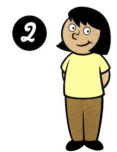

WORKBOOK
page 61

93

Lesson 3

PRACTICE

 1 Color.

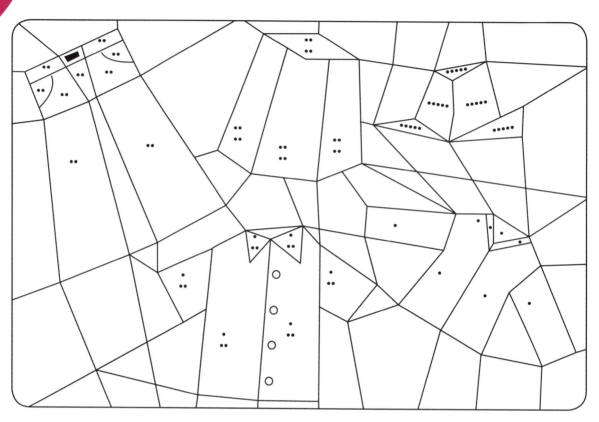

 2 Act out and say.

WORKBOOK page 62

Lesson 4 VOCABULARY

TRACK 83
 1 Listen and point.

TRACK 84
 2 Sing and act out.

Lesson 5

GRAMMAR
It's your (hat).
They're your (shoes).

TRACK 85

1 Listen and point.

 2 Circle and say.

WORKBOOK
page 64

Lesson 6

PRACTICE

 1 Circle and say.

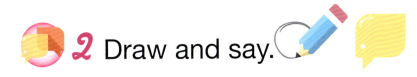 **2** Draw and say.

WORKBOOK page 65

97

Lesson 7

STORY TIME

TRACK 86

 1 Listen and point.

 2 Act out.

 3 Circle the value.

 Be sensible. Wear the right clothes.

98   **WORKBOOK** page 66

Lesson 8

· CRAFT TIME ·

1 Color and make.

2 Show and say.

WORKBOOK page 91

PROGRESS CHECK

1 Say and color.

TRACK 87

2 Listen and number.

STICKERS PASSPORT Page 14

100

PROGRESS CHECK

1 Say and color.

TRACK 88

2 Listen and number.

BOTSWANA

TEAM NAME

1 Get materials.

2 Fold and cut a loom.

3 Cut paper strips.

CHALLENGE 4

PAPER WEAVING

PERU

4 Weave the paper.

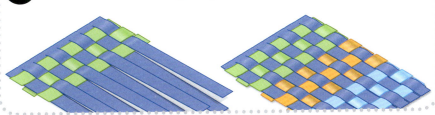

5 Glue.

6 Draw your fabric.

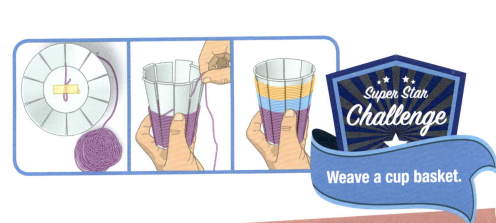

Super Star Challenge
Weave a cup basket.

TEAMWORK

103

WORKBOOK
page 67

Lesson 1

VOCABULARY

TRACK 90

1 Listen and point.

2 Color and say.

106

WORKBOOK page 68

Lesson 2

TRACK 91

1 Listen and point.

> **GRAMMAR**
> I like (salad).
> I don't like (fish).

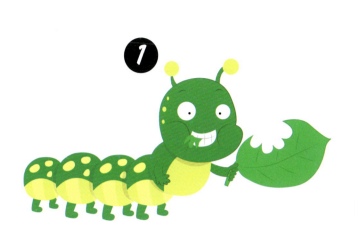

TRACK 92

2 Listen and draw or .

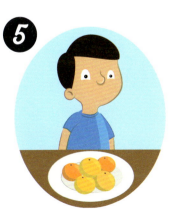

UNIT 9

Lesson 3

PRACTICE

1 Follow and say.

2 Say.

WORKBOOK page 70

Lesson 4 ·VOCABULARY·

TRACK 93

 1 Listen and point.

TRACK 94

 2 Sing and act out.

Lesson 5

GRAMMAR
Do you like (pasta)?
Yes, I do. / No, I don't.

TRACK 95

1 Listen and point.

TRACK 96

 2 Listen and say.

110

WORKBOOK
page 72

Lesson 6

PRACTICE

 1 Listen and draw or .

1

2

3

4

 2 Tell a friend.

WORKBOOK
page 73

111

Lesson 7

TRACK 98

 1 Listen and point.

STORY TIME

 2 Act out.

 3 Circle the value.

Be polite. Say **Please** and **Thank you**.

112

Lesson 8

· CRAFT TIME ·

1 Make a pizza.

2 Play and say.

WORKBOOK
page 75

UNIT 10 Lesson 1

VOCABULARY

TRACK 100

1 Listen and point.

TRACK 101

2 Listen and match.

116

WORKBOOK page 76

Lesson 2

GRAMMAR
I'm in the (bedroom).

TRACK 102

1 Listen and point.

TRACK 103

2 Listen and match.

 1

 2

 3

 4

TRACK 104

  3 Listen and say.

WORKBOOK page 77

117

Lesson 3

PRACTICE

TRACK 105

1 Listen and draw.

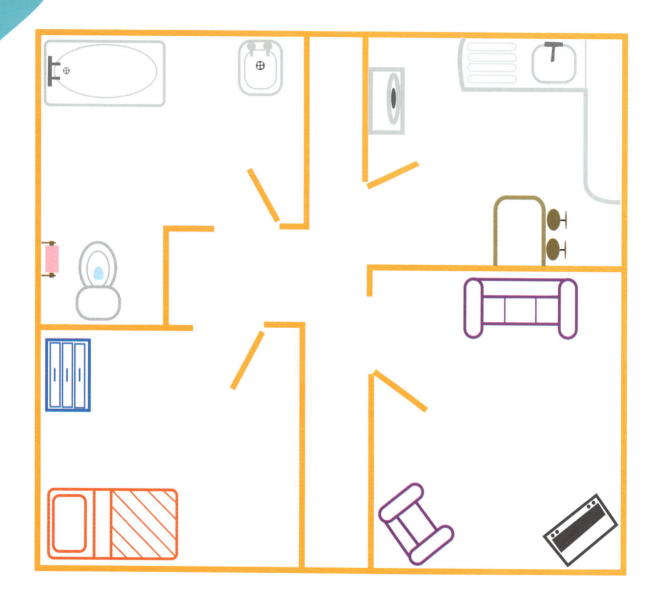

2 Draw and say.

Lesson 4 · VOCABULARY ·

 1 Listen and point.

 2 Sing and act out.

WORKBOOK page 79

MY PICTURE DICTIONARY page 133

119

Lesson 5

GRAMMAR
There's a (bed)
in the (bedroom).

TRACK 108
 1 Listen and point.

TRACK 109
  2 Listen and circle.

120

WORKBOOK page 80

Lesson 6

PRACTICE

1 Circle and say.

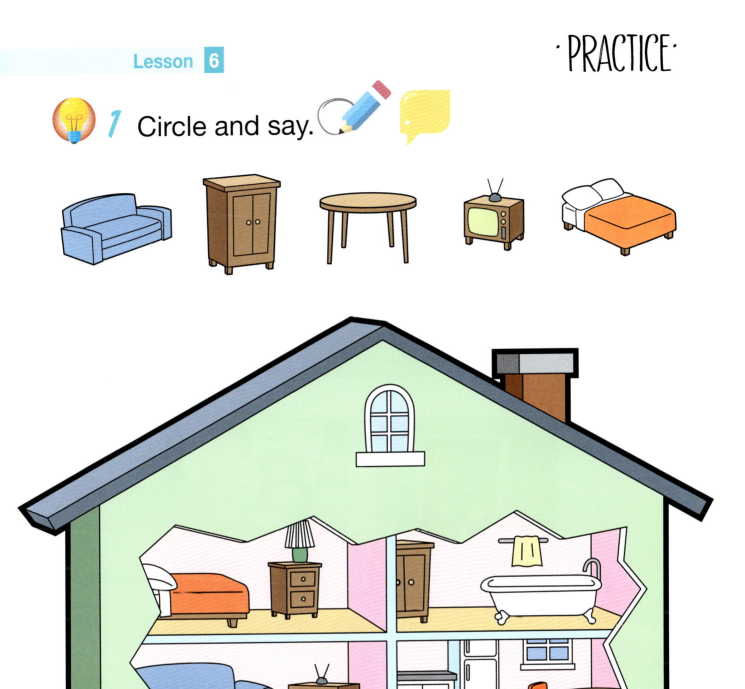

2 Tell a friend.

Lesson 7

STORY TIME

TRACK 110

 1 Listen and point.

 2 Act out.

 3 Circle the value.

 your home.

122

WORKBOOK
page 82

Lesson 8

CRAFT TIME

1 Make a house.

2 Show and say.

WORKBOOK page 93

PROGRESS CHECK

1 Say and color.

 TRACK 111

2 Listen and number.

124

 PROGRESS CHECK

1 Say and color.

TRACK 112

2 Listen and number.

ITALY

TEAM NAME

1 Get materials.

2 Roll your lemon.

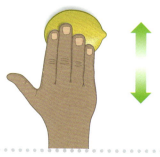

3 Ask an adult to cut it.

126

CHALLENGE 5

MAKE A VOLCANO

USA

4 Add food coloring and dish soap.

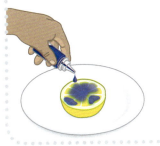 

5 Cover it with baking soda.

6 Make a crater, stir and erupt.

7 Draw your volcano.

Super Star Challenge
Try erupting an orange.

TEAMWORK ★★★★☆

127

MY PICTURE DICTIONARY

133

2020 © Macmillan Education do Brasil

Based on *Next Move* Starter
© Macmillan Publishers Limited 2013
Text © Cantabgilly Limited and Mary Charrington 2013
Picture Dictionary written by Cantabgilly Limited and Mary Charrington 2013
STEAM Challenge sections written by Sarah Elizabeth Sprague
Next Move is a registered trademark, property of Macmillan Publishers, 2013
First edition entitled "Next Stop" published 2009 by Macmillan Publishers

Director of Languages Brazil: Patrícia Souza De Luccia
Publishing Manager and Field Researcher: Patricia Muradas
Content Creation Coordinator: Cristina do Vale
Art Editor: Jean Aranha
Lead Editors: Ana Beatriz da Costa Moreira, Daniela Gonçala da Costa, Luciana Pereira da Silva
Content Editors: Millyane M. Moura Moreira, Tarsílio Soares Moreira
Digital Editor: Ana Paula Girardi
Editorial Intern: Bruna Marques
Art Intern: Jacqueline Alves
Graphic Production: Tatiane Romano, Thais Mendes P. Galvão
Proofreaders: Edward Willson, Márcia Leme, Sabrina Cairo Bileski
Design Concept: Design Divertido Artes Gráficas
Page Make-Up: Figurattiva Editorial
Photo Research: Marcia Sato
Image Processing: Jean Aranha, Jacqueline Alves
Audio: Argila Music, Núcleo de Criação
Cover Concept: Jean Aranha
Cover photography: pmphoto/iStockphoto/Getty Images, Bubert/iStockphoto/Getty Images, LokFung/iStockphoto/Getty Images.
Commissioned photography: Studio8 (p. 11, 12, 17, 22, 24, 27, 38, 41, 46, 51, 60, 63, 65, 70, 73, 75, 84, 89, 94, 99, 108, 113, 123).
Map: Allmaps
Illustrations: Adilson Secco (p. 30-31, 54-55, 78-79, 102-103, 126-127), Chris Embleton | Advocate Art (p. 10, 11, 24, 28, 29, 38, 49, 53, 71, 76, 77, 86, 87, 95, 100, 101, 124, 125), Mike Gelen | Inkwell Studios (p. 13, 24, 36, 45, 48, 61, 72, 73, 84, 92, 93, 96, 110, 111, 120, 121), Bill Ledger (p. 12, 15, 21, 22, 37, 44, 62, 87, 94, 97, 118), Ed Myer | Advocate Art (p. 16, 26, 35, 40, 50, 58, 59, 60, 63, 64, 69, 74, 83, 88, 98, 107, 109, 112, 116, 117, 122, 128, 129, 130, 131, 132, 133), Joseph Wilkins (p. 23, 39, 47, 85, 106).

Reproduction prohibited. Penal Code Article 184 and Law number 9.610 of February 19, 1998.

We would like to dedicate this book to teachers all over Brazil. We would also like to thank our clients and teachers who have helped us make this book better with their many rich contributions and feedback straight from the classroom!

The authors and publishers would like to thank the following for permission to reproduce the photographic material:
p. 8-9: leonello/iStockphoto/Getty Images; p. 10: LightFieldStudios/iStockphoto/Getty Images; p. 14: Paha_L/iStockphoto/Getty Images, Alamy/Fotoarena, aabejon/iStockphoto/Getty Images, andresr/iStockphoto/Getty Images, jaroon/iStockphoto/Getty Images, Toxitz/iStockphoto/Getty Images, klikk/iStockphoto/Getty Images, belchonock/iStockphoto/Getty Images; p. 18: TongRo Images/Easypix, Valeriya/iStockphoto/Getty Images; p. 20: malerapaso/iStockphoto/Getty Images, talipcubukcu/iStockphoto/Getty Images, studo58/iStockphoto/Getty Images, Andrey_Kuzmin/iStockphoto/Getty Images, deepblue4you/iStockphoto/Getty Images; p. 23: design56/iStockphoto/Getty Images, Serg/iStockphoto/Getty Images, lucielang/iStockphoto/Getty Images, studiocasper/iStockphoto/Getty Images, Muralinath/iStockphoto/Getty Images; p. 30: leonello/iStockphoto/Getty Images, phive2015/iStockphoto/Getty Images, 1001Love/iStockphoto/Getty Images, flowgraph/iStockphoto/Getty Images, Boarding1Now/iStockphoto/Getty Images, LeoPatrizi/iStockphoto/Getty Images, Coprid/iStockphoto/Getty Images, karandaev/iStockphoto/Getty Images, DonNichols/iStockphoto/Getty Images, StockPhotosArt/iStockphoto/Getty Images, NicolasMcComber/iStockphoto/Getty Images, NicolasMcComber/iStockphoto/Getty Images, Devonyu/iStockphoto/Getty Images; p. 33: THEPALMER/iStockphoto/Getty Images; p. 34: camacho9999/iStockphoto/Getty Images, epantha/iStockphoto/Getty Images, GlobalP/iStockphoto/Getty Images, dblais4/iStockphoto/Getty Images, RPFerreira/iStockphoto/Getty Images; p. 35: phanuchat/iStockphoto/Getty Images; p. 43: Alamy/Fotoarena; p. 46: hocus-focus/iStockphoto/Getty Images, michaeljung/iStockphoto/Getty Images, Torpee/iStockphoto/Getty Images, Aleks/iStockphoto/Getty Images, erierika/iStockphoto/Getty Images, sunstock/iStockphoto/Getty Images; p. 47: ConstantinosZ/iStockphoto/Getty Images, ElementalImaging/iStockphoto/Getty Images, Brightrock/iStockphoto/Getty Images, pagadesign/iStockphoto/Getty Images, zayatssv/iStockphoto/Getty Images; p. 54: Poligrafistka/iStockphoto/Getty Images, Joel Sartore/Getty Images, Helix Fossil, sharrocks/iStockphoto/Getty Images, KariHoglund/iStockphoto/Getty Images, ksevgi/iStockphoto/Getty Images, Floortje/iStockphoto/Getty Images, Tolga TEZCAN/iStockphoto/Getty Images, StockPhotosArt/iStockphoto/Getty Images; p. 55: Poligrafistka/iStockphoto/Getty Images,

Milehightraveler/iStockphoto/Getty Images, Axel_Valdes/ iStockphoto/Getty Images; p. 56: Alamy/Fotoarena; p. 61: JohnnyGreig/iStockphoto/Getty Images; p. 67: DragonImages/iStockphoto/Getty Images; p. 68: stockyimages/iStockphoto/Getty Images, stocknroll/ iStockphoto/Getty Images, jaroon/iStockphoto/Getty Images, shapecharge/iStockphoto/Getty Images, Ljupco/ iStockphoto/Getty Images, Antonio Diaz/iStockphoto/ Getty Images, praethip/iStockphoto/Getty Images, chengyuzheng/iStockphoto/Getty Images; p. 78: sigurcamp/iStockphoto/Getty Images, powerofforever/ iStockphoto/Getty Images, Marc Dufresne/iStockphoto/ Getty Images, Hemjaa/iStockphoto/Getty Images, Sirichai Asawalapsakul/iStockphoto/Getty Images, nevodka/iStockphoto/Getty Images, Goldfinch4ever/ iStockphoto/Getty Images, Dmytro Skorobogatov/ iStockphoto/Getty Images, Igor Kovalchuk/iStockphoto/ Getty Images, Republica/iStockphoto/Getty Images, Easy Asa/iStockphoto/Getty Images, richcano/iStockphoto/ Getty Images; p. 79: Anastasiia_M/iStockphoto/Getty Images, Photogilio/iStockphoto/Getty Images, Fototrav/ iStockphoto/Getty Images, xuanhuongho/iStockphoto/ Getty Images; p. 81: aghezzi/iStockphoto/Getty Images; p. 82: johan63/iStockphoto/Getty Images, GlobalP/ iStockphoto/Getty Images, GlobalP/iStockphoto/Getty Images, kotomiti/iStockphoto/Getty Images, GlobalP/ iStockphoto/Getty Images, AnitaVDB/iStockphoto/ Getty Images, Rainer von Brandis/iStockphoto/Getty Images, WLDavies/iStockphoto/Getty Images, GlobalP/ iStockphoto/Getty Images, Goddard_Photography/ iStockphoto/Getty Images; p. 85: GlobalP/iStockphoto/ Getty Images, GlobalP/iStockphoto/Getty Images, Tsekhmister/iStockphoto/Getty Images, bazilfoto/ iStockphoto/Getty Images, adogslifephoto/iStockphoto/ Getty Images, colematt/iStockphoto/Getty Images; p. 90-91: The Image Bank/Getty Images; p. 95: baona/ iStockphoto/Getty Images, a-poselenov/iStockphoto/ Getty Images; p. 102: alexsl/iStockphoto/Getty Images, Frans Lanting/Alamy/Fotoarena, Alamy/Fotoarena, Alamy/Fotoarena, CT757fan/iStockphoto/Getty Images, StockPhotosArt/iStockphoto/Getty Images, Muralinath/ iStockphoto/Getty Images, Devonyu/iStockphoto/Getty Images, Eugene4873/iStockphoto/Getty Images, ksevgi/ iStockphoto/Getty Images; p. 103: Ben185/iStockphoto/ Getty Images, Hadynyah/iStockphoto/Getty Images, PacoRomero/iStockphoto/Getty Images; p. 105: Oleh Slobodeniuk/iStockphoto/Getty Images; p. 108: JBryson/ iStockphoto/Getty Images, SergiyN/iStockphoto/Getty Images, LightFieldStudios/iStockphoto/Getty Images, billnoll/iStockphoto/Getty Images, DNY59/iStockphoto/ Getty Images, milanfoto/iStockphoto/Getty Images, nortongo/iStockphoto/Getty Images, ffolas/iStockphoto/ Getty Images, mbongorus/iStockphoto/Getty Images; p. 111: Oleksii Polishchuk/iStockphoto/Getty Images, gbh007/iStockphoto/Getty Images, vikif/iStockphoto/ Getty Images; p. 114: bauhaus1000/iStockphoto/Getty

Images; p. 117: zayatssv/iStockphoto/Getty Images, Believe_In_Me/iStockphoto/Getty Images, laurien/ iStockphoto/Getty Images, Floortje/iStockphoto/ Getty Images, tulcarion/iStockphoto/Getty Images, atiatiati/iStockphoto/Getty Images, ExperienceInteriors/ iStockphoto/Getty Images, Govindanmarudhai/ iStockphoto/Getty Images; p. 119: Artem Perevozchikov/ iStockphoto/Getty Images, urfinguss/iStockphoto/ Getty Images, MicroStockHub/iStockphoto/Getty Images, BahadirTanriover/iStockphoto/Getty Images, Firmafotografen/iStockphoto/Getty Images, Johnny Greig/iStockphoto/Getty Images; p. 124: LokFung/ iStockphoto/Getty Images; p. 126: chokkicx/iStockphoto/ Getty Images, etvulc/iStockphoto/Getty Images, SalvoV/iStockphoto/Getty Images, serebryakova/ iStockphoto/Getty Images, Tnevodka/iStockphoto/Getty Imagesevarak/iStockphoto/Getty Images, Photosbyjam/ iStockphoto/Getty Images, vikif/iStockphoto/Getty Images, Richard Villalo/iStockphoto/Getty Images, Easy_ Asa/iStockphoto/Getty Images, Rosario_82/iStockphoto/ Getty Images; p. 127: Poligrafistka/iStockphoto/ Getty Images, JamesBrey/iStockphoto/Getty Images, joebelanger/iStockphoto/Getty Images, Jim Wiltschko/ iStockphoto/Getty Images.

Dados Internacionais de Catalogação na Publicação (CIP)
Bibliotecária responsável: Aline Graziele Benitez CRB-1/3129

C23n	Cant, Amanda
1.ed.	Next Station Starter: Student's Book / Amanda Cant, Mary Charrington, Sarah Elizabeth Sprague. – 1.ed. – São Paulo: Macmillan Education do Brasil, 2020.
	136 p.; il.; 21 x 27 cm. – (Coleção Next Station)
	ISBN: 978-85-511-0126-1
	1. Língua inglesa. I. Charrington, Mary. II. Sprague, Sarah Elizabeth. III. Título. IV. Série.
	CDD 420

Índice para catálogo sistemático:

1. Língua inglesa

All rights reserved.

MACMILLAN EDUCATION DO BRASIL
Av. Brigadeiro Faria Lima, 1.309, 3° Andar –
Jd. Paulistano – São Paulo – SP – 01452-002
www.macmillan.com.br
Customer Service: [55] (11) 4613-2278
0800 16 88 77
Fax: [55] (11) 4612-6098

Printed in Brazil. Pancrom 10/2023

· MAP STICKERS ·

My House

SOUTH KOREA **IRELAND** **PERU**

BRAZIL **VIETNAM** **ITALY**

MEXICO **BOTSWANA** **USA**

· PASSPORT STICKERS ·